This book belongs to:

official member of the
Be The Change Club.

Joined on:

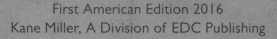

First American Edition 2016
Kane Miller, A Division of EDC Publishing

Copyright © 2016 The Ivy Press Limited

Published by arrangement with Ivy Press Limited, United Kingdom.
All rights reserved. No part of this book may be reproduced,
transmitted or stored in an information retrieval system in any
form or by any means, graphic, electronic or mechanical, including
photocopying, taping and recording, without prior written
permission from the publisher.

For information contact:
Kane Miller, A Division of EDC Publishing
PO Box 470663
Tulsa, OK 74147-0663
www.kanemiller.com
www.edcpub.com
www.usbornebooksandmore.com

Library of Congress Control Number: 2015938831

Printed in China

ISBN: 978-1-61067-404-1

BE THE
CHANGE
MAKE IT
HAPPEN

BY
BERNADETTE RUSSELL

Illustrated by
DAVID BROADBENT

How you
can make a
difference

Kane Miller
A DIVISION OF EDC PUBLISHING

CONGRATULATIONS

Opening this book is the first step toward changing the world. You might not realize it, but you are a hero! You have a lot of power and, like a superhero, you can use your power to take action and make things happen on the issues you really care about.

The suggestions in this book will help you spread the word, fund-raise for important causes, and make a real difference in your community and worldwide. And, most importantly, you'll have lots of fun at the same time!

Your Mission:

Obviously the world is beautiful and full of fun things to do... but do you secretly sometimes wish that you could change a few things? Well, guess what? You don't need a magic wand to transform the world, you just need YOU! Plus:

- A sprinkle of enthusiasm
- A big splash of energy
- This Amazing Book

You can be the superhero the world has been waiting for (with or without a cape. I wear a cape to do my missions, but that's just me).

So, work through this book and by the end you will have transformed into a full-fledged **Change Champion!**

YES! You can do it! You can BE THE CHANGE and MAKE IT HAPPEN!

YOU CAN DO IT!

ANIMAL AWARENESS

You know those posters for missing cats and dogs that you see in parks? Make your own MISSING poster for animals in danger of extinction. For example: MISSING MOUNTAIN GORILLA-only 700 remaining due to shrinking habitat.

Once you've decided on the animals you want to help, research some organizations that help them and put the website details on your poster so people know where to find out more.

Lighten Up

Persuade the grown-ups in your home to change all the regular lightbulbs to energy-saving ones. If they need some encouragement, you can tell them this POLLUTION FACT: if every household in the USA replaced one bulb, that would equal removing 1 MILLION cars from the road.

That'll get them up the ladder! (Reward them with a nice cup of tea and a cookie.)

SILLY SPORTS DAYS

Get a sports committee together with some friends. Each person chooses a silly sport (such as an egg and spoon race, sack race, or juggling).

Hold your sports day in a local park, charging spectators to raise cash for charity. Make trophies for winners out of cardboard that is painted gold, silver, and bronze.

TIP: It's very important for both kids and adults to enjoy being silly.

THE "Seriously, I'm TOO Grown Up For This NOW" SALE

Do you have small sneakers, discarded dolls, or babyish books lying around and tripping you up?

Have a sale and raise some cash for something you care about.

If you have friends and family who also have stuff they don't need, have a GINORMOUS sale.

Pick a favorite charity and send them a letter explaining how you raised the cash—they'll love it!

THE GALLERY OF GOOD CAUSES

Give friends and family a challenge: everyone has one week to create a picture that represents their favorite good cause. They can use any medium of their choice (paints, pens or pencils, a collage, or photographs). Next, put on an exhibition to sell the pictures and invite everyone. Remind visitors that they could be buying the Mona Lisa of the 21st century! Money raised could go to one or all of the causes.

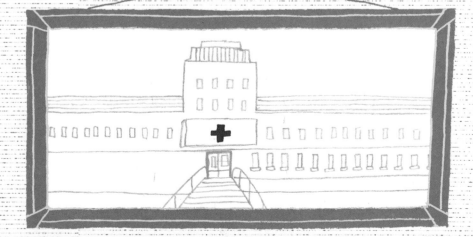

BE A LOCAL STAR

Buy things you need from your local farmers, stores, and markets, and encourage your family and friends to do the same.

This is good because it costs lots of money and uses lots of fuel to import food and other items from miles away. Plus this way you get to know your neighbors and help support local businesses.

IDEA

Why not make the farmers and storekeepers a "thank you for all your hard work" card at the holidays?

Bee The Change

We don't want our bees to BUZZ OFF—we need them! But gardeners have noticed that bees are less healthy and abundant than in the past. Bees fertilize plants by transferring pollen and seeds from one flower to another. When the plant is fertilized, it can grow and produce food. Without bees to spread seeds, many plants would die off.

So plant bee-friendly plants in a garden, on your windowsill, or in any patch of ground you can find! Flowers that bees like include lavender, foxglove, and geraniums.

BZzzzzz

Bees get sluggish in the early morning or late at night. Once the sun comes out they liven up and can fly away. (My sisters are very similar!)

FUN RAISING

Want to raise cash for a good cause? Have a "please-pay-what-you-can" party. For this task, get a group of friends together and each choose a role from this list:

★ **The Host Post:** responsible for making a list of people to invite (and collecting the cash!)
★ **Artsy Fartsy:** in charge of designing the invites and the decoration of the party room
★ **DJ:** in charge of music, including "guest requests," plus lining up a favorite tune from each of the group
★ **Captain Yumyum:** must make sure there's lots of fab food (ask each guest to bring one thing to share)

Give your party a name to match your cause—like "The Tiger Ball" or "Disco for Diabetes."

Grow Your Own

Grow your own veggies, herbs, or salad greens from seed. Growing your own plants will reduce the amount of food being imported, which, in turn, helps to reduce pollution. And many plants thrive in pots. You can easily plant lettuce, tomatoes, and chilies.

IT'S A WRAP

On family birthdays and special occasions, our house is full to the rafters with gift wrap that just gets thrown away. So I've started wrapping presents with recycled paper for less waste. Look around for some old stuff no one wants anymore, such as:

- Maps
- Magazines
- Newspapers
- Sheet music
- Posters
- Wallpaper (but not the paper that's still on your walls!)

Another great idea is to make your own ribbon by cutting strips of old pillowcases or clothes.

My friend Graham often causes mischief by disguising the shape of the gift so you'd never guess what it is...

LONG-LASTING GLASS

Glass takes ONE MILLION years to decompose. (That's older than my Great-aunt Susan!) My kitchen is full of glass jars and this gave me some ideas...

• Create a personalized gift for a friend by decorating a glass jar with his or her name. Use paint made especially for glass. You can make it even prettier if you tie a ribbon around the rim of the jar.

• You can always reuse old jars for storage. Make some cool handwritten labels, such as "thumbtacks" or "dragons' eggs."

Read All About It!

Make your own newspaper! Newspapers can be a bit gloomy, but yours could be full of ideas to help change the world for the better. It can include interviews, stories, and pictures.

Pick a name for your newspaper like "Fun News Doesn't Snooze" or "Happy Times." If you get an adult to photocopy your newspaper, you might sell it to your family and friends and use the money raised for your favorite charity.

Veg Out

Did you know that cattle produce greenhouse gases that contribute to climate change? BUT there's a yummy way to combat this—eat less meat and more delicious veggies!

Vegetable Chili

SERVES 6

- 1 grown-up, to help
- 1 tablespoon olive oil
- 1 chopped onion
- 2 cloves garlic, minced
- 1 chopped green bell pepper
- 4 cups canned pinto beans
- 1 can crushed tomatoes
- 1½ cups canned corn
- 1 minced and seeded chili pepper
- 1 teaspoon dried oregano
- 3 teaspoons chili powder
- 1 teaspoon ground cumin
- A pinch of salt

Method

With an adult's help, heat oil in a large pot. Add onion and sauté over medium heat until onion is golden. Add remaining ingredients. Simmer gently, covered, for 30 minutes, stirring occasionally. If it seems too thick, add ½ cup of water at a time, until it's just the way you like it.

Serve in bowls.

Plastic is NOT Fantastic

Enough plastic is thrown away each year to circle the earth FOUR times!

Here are three things you and your parents can do to help:

❶ Carry a reusable water bottle.
❷ Carry a cloth bag for shopping.
❸ Go digital! No need for plastic DVDs when you can download movies.

Why is Plastic Rubbish?

✳ Plastic takes hundreds of years to decompose.
✳ Our oceans are filling up with it.
✳ Birds mistake this trash for food and it makes them sick!
✳ It can leak bad chemicals into the atmosphere

Growing Up Together

Plant a tree! Why? Because trees provide habitat and food for wildlife, create oxygen for the atmosphere, feed the soil, look nice, and are fun to climb!

You can plant a tree in your yard or even in a park, if you get permission. On the same day of every year, take a photo of you and your friends beside the tree. See how much we all grow!

REMEMBER
You can grow trees from seeds (acorns or chestnuts) so you don't need to spend any money!

NIFTY THRIFTY

Donate your clothes to a charity or resale store so someone else can use them. Then you can buy something someone else doesn't need anymore. Lots of clothes get outgrown but still look like new. Plus, buying secondhand is cheaper so there might be money left over for fun activities like swimming or space travel. (OK, maybe not quite enough for that last one.) Other places you can get super secondhand stuff are garage sales, flea markets, and online marketplaces.

MAGIC iN THE MUD

Next to my house was a patch of muddy brown yuckiness filled with trash. We cleared all the trash away and sprinkled wildflower seeds over the ground. Like magic, a few weeks later that ugly patch was beautiful and filled with color. (The fun part was overhearing people talking about it. We do it everywhere now!)

And the flowers create a haven for bees, butterflies, and other wildlife.

With an adult helper, try this in your neighborhood. Don't forget to ask for permission first!

Boys Like Baking & Girls Like Dinosaurs!

Some people think boys and girls only like certain things. For example, boys like cars and girls like cooking, but I don't think that's true!

Gather two groups with equal numbers of boys and girls. Each group writes a list of their top ten favorite things in the world, then reads the list to the other group. I guarantee there'll be some surprises—in my group, half of the boys liked baking and all the girls wanted a pet dinosaur.

This may not sound like a world-changing exercise, but changing how people think does really make a difference!

SUPER

HELP! The world needs you to turn it into a nicer place! For this mission, you will need some willing friends/relatives.

1 Help each other invent superhero names, like Captain Hugtastic (good at hugging) or Trashgirl (great at clearing up rubbish) and then a name for the group like "The Superkids League."

HEROES

2 Decide on all the things your group would like to do to make the world a better place. Then decide who does what. (Captain Hugtastic could cheer people up with hugs.)

3 Make some superhero capes using old towels or blankets, and make a mask for everyone. Anytime you need inspiration, gather your friends for a meeting, and wear your capes!

THE TOYS ARE REVOLTING!

Make mini placards from recycled cards, and craft sticks and create a mini protest with your toys to highlight issues you care about. The placards can say things like:

DRIVE LESS

WALK MORE!

The protest can go on display in a windowsill or
on a table so people can see it and be inspired.

FLYING YOUR FLAG

Design a beautiful flag out of a recycled sheet or pillowcase. You'll need acrylic paints or permanent markers. Write something inspirational on your flag like "Let's Make Our World Even Better Together."

Look at other flags and think about what colors and designs would work for your message.

Hang it where people can see it. In your window or on a pole in your yard would be great places.

TRASHTASTIC

Too much trash just goes to landfills, but my Auntie Carol makes amazing sculptures out of all sorts of materials. Maybe you could get artsy and make something amazing and beautiful out of trash, too?

Your challenge is to create a sculpture out of trash for display at home, then make a sign for it explaining what it is.

If you do this project with some neighbors, you can even have a rubbish exhibition.

Look for things like cardboard, plastic, aluminum foil, and paper.

RUBBISH ROBOT

RADIO DAYS

In the olden days if you wanted to share your ideas, you had to write a letter and send it by horse and it'd take weeks to arrive. Now you can just record your own radio show! Interview your friends about activities you've been doing to change the world, and experiment with fun sound effects (try dried peas for rain or coconut shells for hooves).

Borrow an adult's cell phone to record yourselves, then e-mail it or invite friends over to listen. Everyone hearing about your mission will be inspired!

NEWSFLASH

Make a TV out of an old cardboard box. Write and rehearse a pretend news show with a few stories.

Some examples could be "Local charity shop is looking for donations" or "Rain forests need our help."

Find a name for your station like "Channel Change." Then broadcast your show live to friends and family from inside the cardboard TV. Maybe even film it (borrowing an adult's cell phone) and share the video with them.

The World is a Rainbow

I love that there are so many different people in the world. I have Nigerian, Irish, Turkish, Indian, and Russian neighbors, which I think we should celebrate!

Trace around your hand, then color it in any color that you like. Ask your friends and family to join in and start to make a rainbow of the hands. Place it in a window where everyone can see it to remind them that we are all people, no matter what color we are.

The Happiness Diary

Some people get sad more easily than others, but thinking positively can help. Even if you don't get sad often, thinking positively is always a good thing! So write down three things every day in a happy diary:

1. Something I thought was beautiful.
2. Something that made me happy.
3. Something I am thankful for.

After a week, read it through. If you like it, keep writing! It's a good habit to get into. Not a bad habit like biting your toenails. (Not that I do that... much.)

A Beautiful World

If people notice what is beautiful about the world, I think they are more likely to want to take care of it. So write a list of what is beautiful—it might rhyme, but it's OK if it doesn't. This is actually a really cool way of writing a poem. When you've finished, you can keep it somewhere for inspiration, or read it aloud to your family and friends, or copy it and give it to someone (especially if they feel sad).

Here's mine:

I like seeing shapes in the clouds in the sky
I like eating apple and strawberry pie
I like walking my dog for miles and miles
I like my sister's happy smile
I like the sun and I like the rain
I like visiting my mom at the seaside by train
Life is wonderful!

HEROES

We've already talked about superheroes-they are obviously cool. But there are everyday heroes in our lives who are just as important because they give us someone to look up to and make the world a better place. They just wear regular clothes though and don't get lots of attention. Think about who in your life is your hero and write down why. Then tell them! They will be happy to be appreciated and you'll have the bonus of making a great person smile.

My hero is my mom who is funny and kind every day.

COMIC CAPERS

Create your own "Be The Change" comic. Write a simple story about a super way of changing the world for the better in a maximum of nine sentences. Divide a page into squares to match the number of sentences, then tell your story with pictures, plus word and thought bubbles. (Check out some comics to see how it's done.) You might sell your finished comic as a fund-raiser for your favorite charity. Kapow!

STORY Banners

Use banners to tell everyone about "Be the change!" Get some blank postcards, clothespins, string, pens, and crafty stuff for decorating. Carefully write out B-E-T-H-E-C-H-A-N-G-E, putting one letter on each postcard. On the other side, write something you've done to make it happen, then go wild decorating until it's the Greatest Banner Ever (you can do it!). Pin the letters to string and display where it can be admired on both sides!

Rope in some friends to help. You could do it yourself, but it might take a month and your hand would get tired from so much writing.

HOME CINEMA

Organize a movie night. Sell tickets plus popcorn, candy, and ice cream. Invite as many people as you can fit in to your house, being careful not to squash any small visitors. All funds raised can go to charity. You can try to match the movie with the charity in some way. Why not start a regular movie club once a month to raise money for a good cause?

The speaking spoon

Get a wooden spoon. Everyone gets to choose something they want to debate for up to two minutes. While they hold the "speaking spoon" nobody can interrupt them until they've finished. Afterward, they hand the spoon to anyone who has a question, but only the person holding the spoon can talk. The speaking spoon is a good way of resolving arguments.

Gandhi (who was from India and extremely wise) said:

"Be the change you wish to see in the world."

This is super good advice. Lots of wise people have said clever things over the years, but I kept forgetting what they said. So I made a "Little Book Of Wisdom" and every time someone says something good/clever/inspiring I write it in the book. I read it if I am feeling a bit lost or confused. Why not start one for yourself?

Little Book
of Wisdom

Other examples of wise words:

"Think happy, be happy."
Anonymous

"No act of kindness is ever wasted."
Aesop

"Most problems are solved with ice cream and a hug."
My sister

THEY CAME FROM OUTER SPACE

WITH A BUNCH OF FRIENDS, MAKE A LITTLE SHOW
PRETENDING TO BE AN ALIEN FROM ANOTHER PLANET,
VISITING EARTH FOR THE FIRST TIME AND NOTICING
ALL THE AMAZING THINGS ABOUT IT. PRACTICE,
THEN PERFORM YOUR SHOW, WITH FACE
MAKEUP AND WACKY ALIEN COSTUMES,
REMINDING YOUR AUDIENCE HOW
AMAZING THE WORLD IS AND HOW
WE SHOULD TAKE CARE OF IT.

The Pledge

Get adults and kids in your neighborhood to take the "Be The Change" pledge. On a piece of paper write: "We promise to do everything we can to make the world a better place." Ask people to sign their names. Get everyone to write one thing that they will do that week next to their name. You can give them suggestions too:

Walk instead of drive, plant a tree, think positive thoughts...

You get the idea!

Wishes for The World

Collect some twigs and arrange them in a vase.
On luggage tags, write what you wish for the
world. For example, "I wish everyone had enough to
eat" or "I wish no one was cruel to animals," then
tie the tags onto the twigs. Make a sign saying:
"This is our Wish Tree, with all the things we wish
for the world. Please add yours." Place it somewhere
that people will see it, like an after-school club
or community center.

My friend Tony, his son, and their dog "Silly Dog," are always eating fruit (they are a very healthy family), so when they're out walking, they plant the seeds from the fruit wherever they are. You might think they wouldn't grow, but Tony says they've seen two apple trees as a result of their walk planting. Whenever you have seeds or pits left over from fruit like plums, peaches, or apples, start planting! Go back in a year and see what has happened.

An Apple A Day

Check with a grown-up first that it is ok to plant the seed in the place you have chosen.

The Society of Silliness

Seriously now, silliness is EXTREMELY important. Get your whole family to be silly for the day. Everyone must do a silly walk, a silly voice, a silly song, and then finish it up with a silly party where you have to do a silly dance to a selection of silly songs chosen by all.

This whole thing may seem, ahem, silly, but I guarantee there'd be much less arguing in the world if everyone took more time to be silly.

crazy cat

Silly = Happy!

Love
CAN CHANGE THE WORLD

If you love someone, then make sure you
tell him or her. It's easy to forget to do
this, but they will be very pleased
if you remember.

TIPS FOR THE SHY AND BASHFUL
Ok, actually saying it might be embarrassing, or maybe you don't see them that often.
So draw a heart and send it to them or leave it somewhere they'll find it.

SAY SOMETHING
NICE

Don't get caught up in saying mean things about people—everyone has something good about him or her. Sometimes mean or grumpy people are the ones most in need of a kind word. Next time you find yourself annoyed with someone, think of something nice to say to them—congratulate them on something they're good at ("Your drawings are awesome!") or give them a compliment ("Great jacket!").

NICENESS CAN CHANGE THE WORLD.

GREAT JACKET

MY PERFECT WORLD

I think our imaginations are the most powerful tools we have to create change. So write down your idea of a perfect world and explain how you would fix all the things you think are wrong!

Then read it to your family and friends, or at school or a club. You don't need to learn it, just make sure you've practiced reading it out loud. You'll get people to think about their own ideas!

(My sister said in hers there'd be chocolate growing on trees...)

Fashion Show

Use your creative talents and organize a fashion show. Choose recycled clothes and fabrics and invite everyone you know to see your gorgeous designs. You can charge an entrance fee or sell the clothes to raise some funds. For inspiration, look at cat-walk pictures—some of them are pretty wild, so you can go for it! And check out the way the models walk. Very snazzy. Practice your walk and strut your stuff.

HATS THE WAY TO DO IT

Sometimes people temporarily lose their hair when they are being treated for cancer— they can feel shy about it, plus get chilly when it's cold!

Ask everyone you know to donate hats, for kids and adults, and take your collection to a local hospital.

Make a "feel better soon" card for the whole ward. Ask everyone who donates to sign it.

PHOTO-INSPIRATION ALBUM

Borrow a camera, and get some pens and cardboard. Then ask friends to write a promise on the cardboard, such as "I'll walk to school every day." Hold it in front of them and snap! Take as many pictures as possible, print them out for display, and share them with your friends.

High five hello!

No one can resist a high five. If you see someone looking a bit sad, or bored, or lonely, even if you don't know him or her, offer a high five. If they don't know how to do one (like my friend Fred), you can teach them. Fred now high-fives with EVERYONE!

TIP: Go easy on the slap though. Not too hard.

Let It All Out!

Some people bottle up their anger and then it comes out in a burst. This is not good for peace in the world or people with sensitive ears. But it's ok to be angry sometimes—we all have those days. So you can do a "controlled explosion." With a friend, or Mom and Dad, go somewhere you can have a big shout and let it out! You'll feel lots better. If other people see you, tell them what you were doing (in case they were scared).

WATER WORLD

These days there are more of us, but the same amount of water. So obviously saving water is a Good Thing. Try this: make fun speech bubble signs encouraging everyone to save water in lots of different ways, such as:

Above faucets "TURN ME OFF!"
On washing machines "FILL ME UP!"
On leaky faucets "FIX ME!"
In your yard "GIVE ME A RAIN BARREL!"

The grown-ups will probably smile at this, and hopefully do something. You can keep an eye on them.

The Kids' Party

Kids must make their voices heard! You can't vote or make laws—but you can share your ideas and talk about what you think is right. Write a speech about what you would do if you were president of the country. Include new laws you'd make, and changes you would bring about. Present your speech to the adults in your family (it might make them think).

Send your BOOKS around the WORLD

Books are FANTASTIC—great for fun and for finding out all sorts of things. When you've outgrown some of yours, you can donate them to a thrift shop or resale store. Write a message inside each book saying, "When you've read this, please pass it on." Your book could get passed around the world...

Or you can use an organized project to send your books to people who wouldn't ordinarily be able to get books. Take a look online to find out about various projects that run this service.

when life gives you lemons...

...make lemonade! A lemonade stand outside your house is a fantabulous way to raise money for your favorite cause.

RECIPE
1 grown-up to help
9-10 large lemons
2½ cups SUPERFINE sugar
8 cups water

1. SQUEEZE those lemons until you have about 2 cups of juice. 2. SHAKE 3 cups of water and all the sugar together (remembering to put the lid on your container first). 3. strain the lemon juice. Add it to the rest of the water, then pop into the fridge. YUM! 4. cover a table in a bright cloth for your stand and make a sign saying: "when life gives you lemons, make lemonade—or buy ours!"

The OLD Ones Are The BEST

There's a lot to be learned from older people. They've been around longer and can know a lot more than younger people.

There are lots of good ways you can help them through volunteering, but the best of all is taking time to listen. They always have good stories. You can learn a lot of cool stuff from seniors that you wouldn't find in a book. Don't be afraid to ask.

KIDS ARE HEROES

Be inspired by other kids!

You might ask, "What can I do? I'm just a kid." I say, "Anything!" Here are some hero kids from around the world. There's a space in there waiting for you.

Brandon Keefe, collecting books for children's homes

Olivia Taylor, raising funds and awareness for the environment

Malala Yousafzai, campaigning for education rights

YOU!

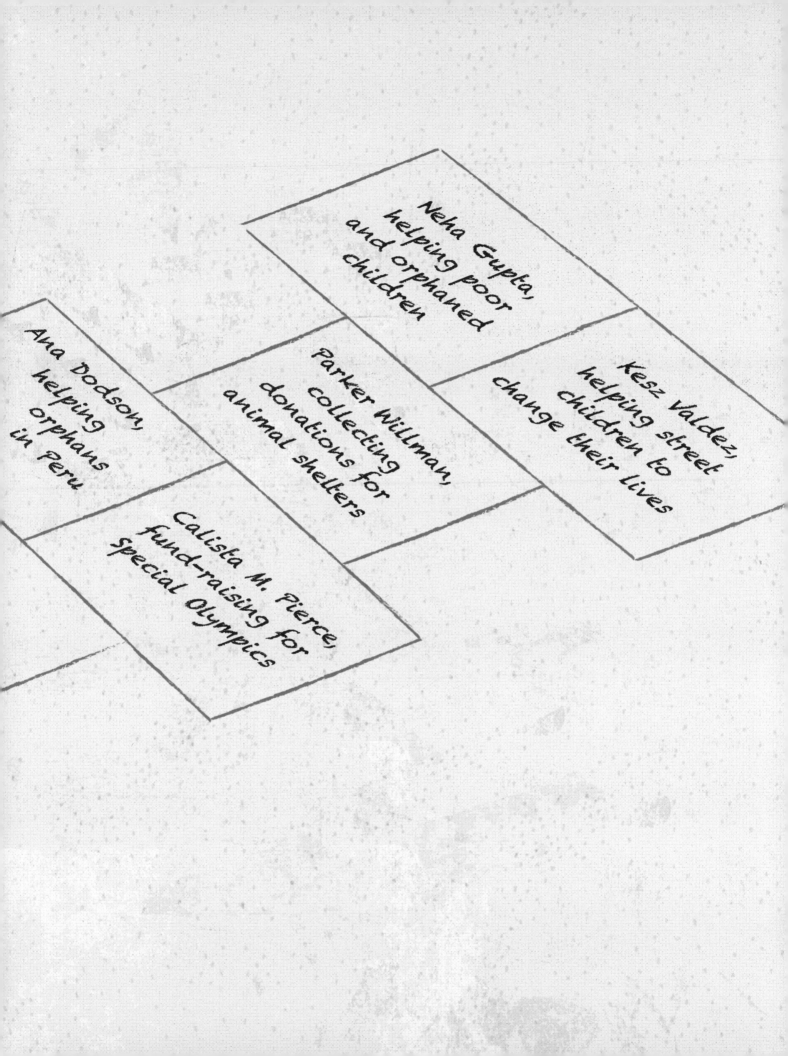

Hello, neighbor!

A wonderful way of making the world a better place is simple: getting to know each other better and being friendlier. So here's an idea. Make postcards for ten people on your street who you don't know very well. Draw pictures on the postcard and write something like, "Hello, we are your neighbors from 36a. We hope that you like living on this street. We hope to see you soon. If you see us, please wave." I bet that'll work.

MY HOME HAS GOT TALENT

Let everyone show off their voices or musical skills and raise money at the same time by putting on a concert at home. You can go solo with a backing track, play your favorite piece of piano/kazoo/tuba music, or perform a song with your friends. Make sure to charge for entrance and most importantly, clap and cheer for everyone so they all feel wonderful! It's a win-win situation!

THANK YOU DAY

Create your own "Thank You Day."

You could say "Thanks, mom, for being patient with me when I nearly make us late" or "Thank you for being my friend because it makes me happy."

It's free to say thank you and makes people feel warm and fuzzy. Encourage others to join you, then everywhere you go, you'll hear people saying "THANK YOU" and see them smiling.

HANDS UP

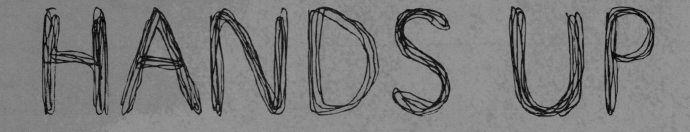

volunteering is great for helping people, making new friends, and having fun. Things you can do include: feeding animals at a shelter, visiting kids in the hospital, being a reader for blind people, delivering food to seniors, cleaning up a wildlife reserve... decide what you'd like to do and ask a grown-up to help you investigate what's in your local area.

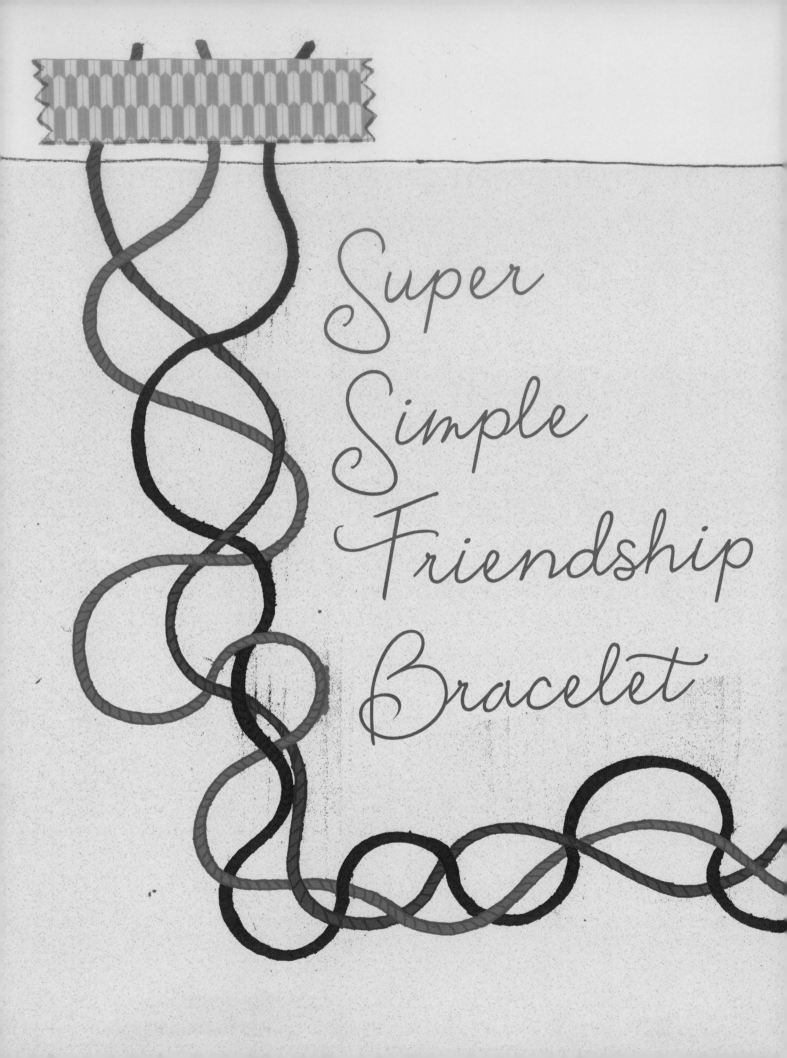

Super Simple Friendship Bracelet

*Your friends make the world a better place
—so let them know they're special!*

Get some yarn in three great colors.

1 Cut three 10-inch lengths, one of each color.

2 Knot them together at the top and tape the knot to a table to keep it steady. Fan out the three strands.

3 Start braiding! Fold the left thread over the center thread, then the right thread over the center thread and repeat, until you have a neatly braided multicolored bracelet.

4 Knot it at the end and cut off any straggly ends. It's now ready. Your friend can wear it around their wrist however they like.

Sweet Calculations

First, wash out a jar, the biggest one you can find. Next, fill it with yummy candy, counting as you put it in. Then, challenge your friends to guess the quantity in the jar and charge them for each guess. The nearest guess after 20 guesses wins the jar, and gets to choose a good cause to receive the money.

Telling Tales

TVs and computers are fun, but sometimes they can turn us into a bunch of mumbling zombies. For a change, switch off the TV and put all electronic devices away. Gather the whole family, then try telling a story, with one person saying one sentence at a time. Spending time doing something together is fun, plus it could turn out to be the Best Story of All Time.

"Be The Change"

AWARDS

Hold your own awards ceremony-you can make a red carpet out of a roll of red paper and some statues out of cardboard spray-painted gold.

Categories could include:
* Person who was kindest to animals
* Person who did most for kids
* Person who did the most recycling

Invite your friends and family or, if you get permission, hold it at school.

WITH ONE FOOTSTEP...

Walking instead of driving is good for your health and for the planet. Encourage your whole family to walk as much as possible. Each month, keep a record of how many miles you have each walked and add it all together. If it's a larger number than the previous month, award yourselves a prize!

(Maybe ice cream. Then you could walk it off.)

Love your Librarian

Books can change the world. They teach us, make us laugh, and inspire us. Librarians take care of books and make sure we have access to them for free, which is amazing.

Make your librarian a little homemade book, explaining why you love the library and what books you enjoy most. Not all heroes leap over buildings, remember. Librarians are quiet heroes.

Never forget the quiet heroes!

Going, going, GONE!

ORGANIZE A FUND-RAISING AUCTION.

1. Collect donations like toys or other things people no longer want.
2. Invite friends and family with a list of all the great stuff on offer.
3. Hold your auction.

The auctioneer should say:
"This cake starts at $1, do I have $2? Good, do I have $3?"
When no one wants to bid higher, they say "going, going, gone—to Suzy Sponge* for $10."

* Or whomever...

Good Gifts

Next time you have a
birthday party, ask
your guests to bring a
small gift to donate to a
children's hospital. You can
also do this at holiday time. Invite
everyone to wrap an extra present
to donate to shelters, retirement homes
or children's homes. Be sure to make a tag
for the present saying, "Happy Birthday/
Christmas/Holidays, with love from (your name)."

PRESENTS for PETS

Animal shelters always need extra food. You can help by asking your friends and neighbors—especially people you know who are pet owners—to donate a can of pet food.

Other ways you can assist shelters is by helping to walk the dogs or fostering animals before they find their forever homes. Find out what your local shelter needs.

In their SHOES...

ONE CHALLENGING THING FOR HOMELESS PEOPLE IS HAVING BAD SHOES. WET AND PAINFUL FEET ARE VERY DIFFICULT IF YOU SPEND MOST OF YOUR TIME OUTSIDE. COLLECT SHOES IN GOOD CONDITION FOR HOMELESS PEOPLE: BIG GROWN-UP SIZES ARE BEST. FIND OUT WHERE YOUR LOCAL HOSTELS AND SHELTERS ARE AND DELIVER SHOES THERE. YOU WILL HAVE MADE SOMEONE'S LIFE MUCH EASIER...

The Story of You

Read your friend/family member a story in bed, but surprise them by replacing one of the character names with their name, to make them feel special. You could also write a story especially for them. Everyone loves being read to—you could even offer to read stories to kids in the hospital, or to your parents to repay them for reading to you.

Go Green!

Get an old T-shirt, and with a thick pen write eco tips like:

1. Switch off faucets
2. Turn off lights
3. Use less plastic
4. Walk, don't drive

Then, using face paint, give yourself a green face. People will definitely ask you why you're green, then you can teach them all you've learned about how to be a friend to the environment.

LITTER LEGENDS

Litter is bad. It can hurt wild animals and birds, blow into traffic, and pollute the environment.

So, become a litter legend. Get together with some friends and see who can fill the most bags!

Identify somewhere that is really full of litter and see how many bags you can fill. When I went litter collecting with some friends, we left a sign nearby saying "Keep it Tidy—Litter Legends Were Here!"

I'm Sorry

Sometimes I'm grouchy. That's OK, it's just being human (or maybe I've turned into a monster. Mmm).

If you've been mean/naughty/grumpy, or think you should say sorry then say it. Make a habit of saying sorry, and forgiving other people when they do something wrong. You'll feel better, and you'll be contributing to Peace In The World.

GOOD FOR YOU!

Kindness.

There's a saying "No act of kindness, however small, is ever wasted." I reckon that's true. Try to be kind as often as possible. Help people carry shopping bags. Help Mom and Dad with chores. Help your brother or sister with their homework. Be nice to everyone you meet. And be kind to yourself. Kindness can definitely change the world.

HAIR TODAY, GONE TOMORROW.

CHALLENGE A TEACHER/PARENT/YOUTH LEADER TO SHAVE FOR A GOOD CAUSE. YOU CAN CHARGE PEOPLE A FEE TO WATCH IT HAPPEN. WHERE I LIVE, ALMOST EVERYONE HAS A BEARD, SO I ORGANIZED A "BEARD-ATHON" AND TEN OF MY FRIENDS SHAVED THEIR BEARDS OFF FOR CHARITY.

PS. THEY COULD ALSO SHAVE THEIR HAIR OFF, BUT REMEMBER TO BUY THEM A HAT OR THEY'LL GET CHILLY.

ODD BOD'S ODD JOBS

Offer to do chores for people who might need help, for free. Write down the stuff you'll do on a list like this:

- Washing dishes
- Raking leaves
- Feeding the cat while they're away

**To make it more fun, I dress up when I do the odd job.
It livens up dishwashing!**

BACKYARD COMPOST

Composting is good because it reduces waste in landfills and improves the soil for our plants.

❶ Pick a spot away from direct sunlight.

❷ Turn a plastic bin upside down and cut out a lid.

❸ Add 1 part nitrogen (grass, coffee grounds/tea bags, fruit/veg scraps) to 3 parts carbon (leaves, straw, cardboard).

❹ It should be damp (not wet). Leave uncovered on a rainy day if it dries out.

❺ Give it a stir now and then in the summer.

❻ When it looks like soil, dig it into your garden and let the plants enjoy!

TREASURE CHEST

Put some "treasure" (drawings, books, etc) in an old box and hide it. Then create a treasure hunt for your friends. Draw a map and leave clues, such as sticky notes saying "nearly there" or chalk arrows on the sidewalk.

Everyone who plays has to donate something they don't use anymore, like an old toy, which you can give to charity afterward.

FUNNY FACE COMPETITION

This competition comes in two rounds. Everyone makes a small donation to enter. First, the kids judge the adults and decide who can make the silliest face. Then the adults judge the kids. When there's a kid and a grown-up winner, they have to compete for "overall winner." The money can go to your favorite good cause. Remember to take photos!

Recycled Greetings

Make greeting cards for friends and family out of recycled materials. Get your parents to save cardboard boxes, magazines, fabric, and other stuff you can use to make beautiful cards.

Here's one I made with buttons for eyes, string for a mouth, words cut out of an old magazine to spell out M-O-M, all glued onto cardboard from an old shoe box and colored in.

The
BEST
Things in Life
ARE FREE

Draw some dollar bills with a picture of you on them, but instead of writing "1 dollar" on them, write "1 favor." Give these to friends and family as gifts. When they hand their notes over, you have to do one favor for them, such as clean their bike. So it's basically a gift certificate, but it doesn't cost you any real money. Neat!

MAKE A LIST OF THE TOP TEN CAUSES OR
CHARITIES THAT ARE IMPORTANT TO YOU.

THINK ABOUT WHICH ACTIVITY YOU
COULD DO TO HELP OR RAISE MONEY
FOR EACH OF YOUR TOP TEN CAUSES.

KEEP A RECORD OF WHAT YOU DO, AND
WHEN YOU HAVE DONE SOMETHING FOR EACH
ONE, GIVE YOURSELF A MASSIVE CHEER! (PLUS
REMEMBER TO DO A CELEBRATORY DANCE.)

Websites

To donate your books to other kids who need them:
Books For Africa
www.booksforafrica.org

International Book Project
www.intlbookproject.org

Little Free Library
www.littlefreelibrary.org

To find out about amazing stuff that other kids have done:
Kids Are Heroes
www.kidsareheroes.org

To learn more about nature and how you can help the earth:
Earth's Kids Kids Club
www.earthskids.com/kidsclub.aspx

To help other kids' get the opportunities they deserve:
Kids Change The World
www.kidschangetheworld.org

To get active in your community:
FreeChild Project
www.freechild.org/youth_activism_2.htm

To find out about your rights as a kid and how to stand up for the rights of your fellow kids:
Save The Children
www.savethechildren.org

To find out how to grow veggies, plant a bee-friendly garden and get green fingers:
Kids Gardening
www.kidsgardening.org

To find out more about recycling:
Recycling
www.benefits-of-recycling.com/recyclingforkids

To find out more about bullying and how you can stop it:
Stop Bullying
www.stopbullying.gov

To find more ways to help our animal friends:
Peta Kids
www.petakids.com

To read about other inspirational kids who have Changed The World, and to see how you could nominate someone for the Peace Prize:
Children's Peace Prize
www.childrenspeaceprize.org

Although every endeavor has been made by the publisher to ensure that all content from these websites is age appropriate, we strongly advise that Internet access is supervised by a responsible adult.